Marsupials
Kangaroos

by Natalie Deniston

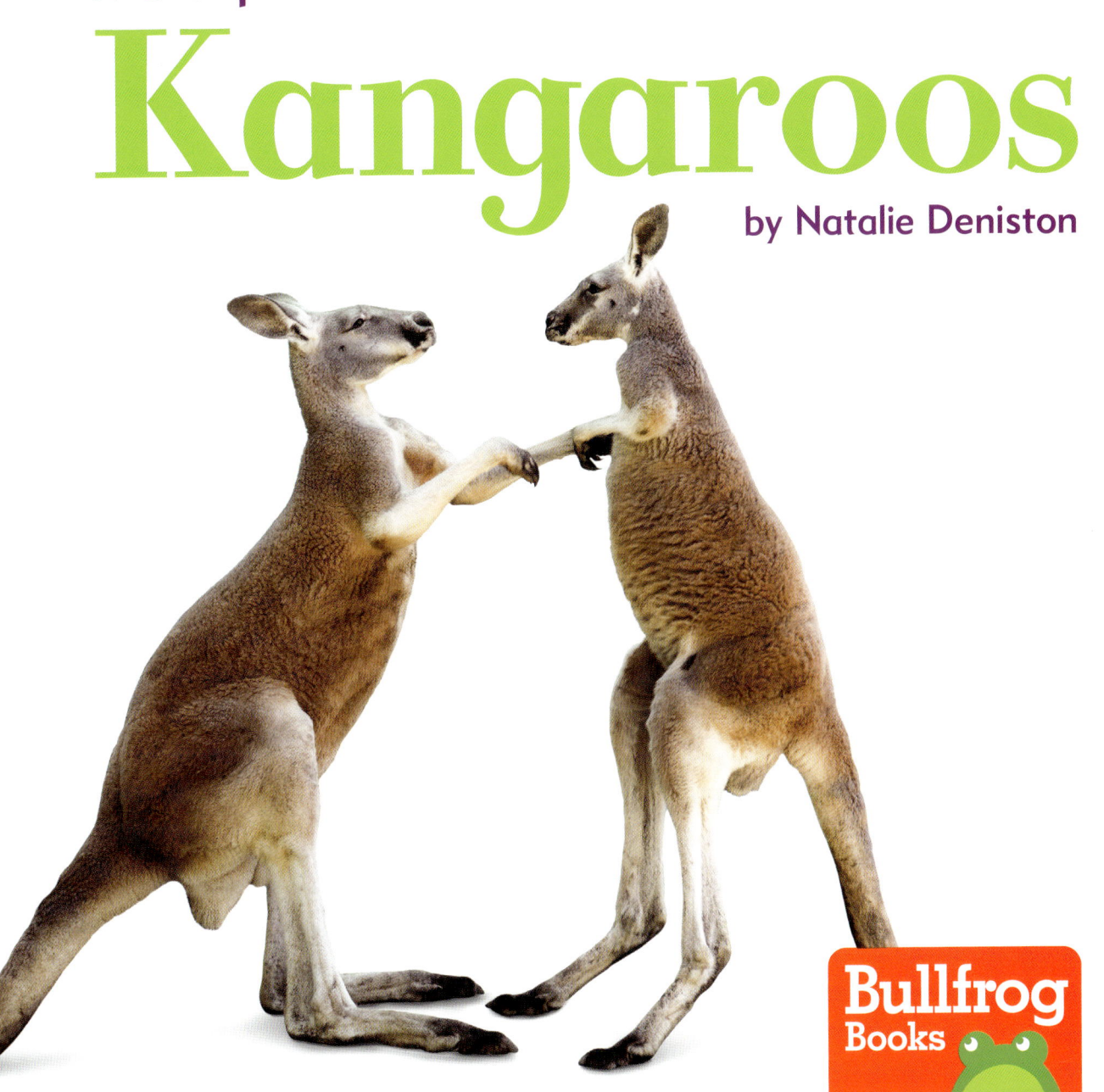

Bullfrog Books

Ideas for Parents and Teachers

Bullfrog Books let children practice reading informational text at the earliest reading levels. Repetition, familiar words, and photo labels support early readers.

Before Reading
- Discuss the cover photo. What does it tell them?
- Look at the picture glossary together. Read and discuss the words.

Read the Book
- "Walk" through the book and look at the photos. Let the child ask questions. Point out the photo labels.
- Read the book to the child, or have them read independently.

After Reading
- Prompt the child to think more. Ask: Kangaroos are marsupials. Moms have pouches. Can you name any other marsupials?

Bullfrog Books are published by Jump!
5357 Penn Avenue South
Minneapolis, MN 55419
www.jumplibrary.com

Copyright © 2025 Jump! International copyright reserved in all countries. No part of this book may be reproduced in any form without written permission from the publisher.

Library of Congress Cataloging-in-Publication Data

Names: Deniston, Natalie, author.
Title: Kangaroos / by Natalie Deniston.
Description: Minneapolis, MN: Jump!, Inc., [2025]
Series: Marsupials | Includes index.
Audience: Ages 5–8
Identifiers: LCCN 2024020200 (print)
LCCN 2024020201 (ebook)
ISBN 9798892135160 (hardcover)
ISBN 9798892135177 (paperback)
ISBN 9798892135184 (ebook)
Subjects: LCSH: Kangaroos—Juvenile literature.
Classification: LCC QL737.M35 D46 2025 (print)
LCC QL737.M35 (ebook)
DDC 599.2/22—dc23/eng/20240506
LC record available at https://lccn.loc.gov/2024020200
LC ebook record available at https://lccn.loc.gov/2024020201

Editor: Katie Chanez
Designer: Emma Almgren-Bersie

Photo Credits: Bradley Blackburn/Shutterstock, cover; volkova natalia/Shutterstock, 1; Benny Marty/Shutterstock, 3; Freder/iStock, 4; JohnCarnemolla/iStock, 5, 19; Christopher Meder/Shutterstock, 6–7; newboy112/iStock, 8; tracielouise/iStock, 9, 23tr; Auscape International Pty Ltd/Alamy, 10–11, 23bl; AlecTrusler2015/Shutterstock, 12–13, 23br; Stephanie Jackson-Australian wildlife collection/Alamy, 14–15, 23bm; Martin Pelanek/Shutterstock, 16–17, 23tl; ice_blue/Shutterstock, 18, 23tm; Jean-Paul Ferrero/Mary Evans Picture Library/SuperStock, 20–21; Smileus/Shutterstock, 22; Naoto Shinkai/Shutterstock, 24.

Printed in the United States of America at Corporate Graphics in North Mankato, Minnesota.

Table of Contents

Hop!	4
Parts of a Kangaroo	22
Picture Glossary	23
Index	24
To Learn More	24

Hop!

Hop! Hop!

A kangaroo hops.

Big feet help.

So does a long tail.

tail

Kangaroos live in forests.

They live by grass, too.
They eat it.

A joey is born.
It is tiny.
It drinks milk.

It grows.

It is safe in Mom's pouch.

The joey gets too big for the pouch!

It comes out.

It joins the mob.

Two kangaroos fight.
They box.

A dingo hunts.

Hop away!

The days are hot.
They sleep.

Parts of a Kangaroo

What are the parts of a kangaroo? Take a look!

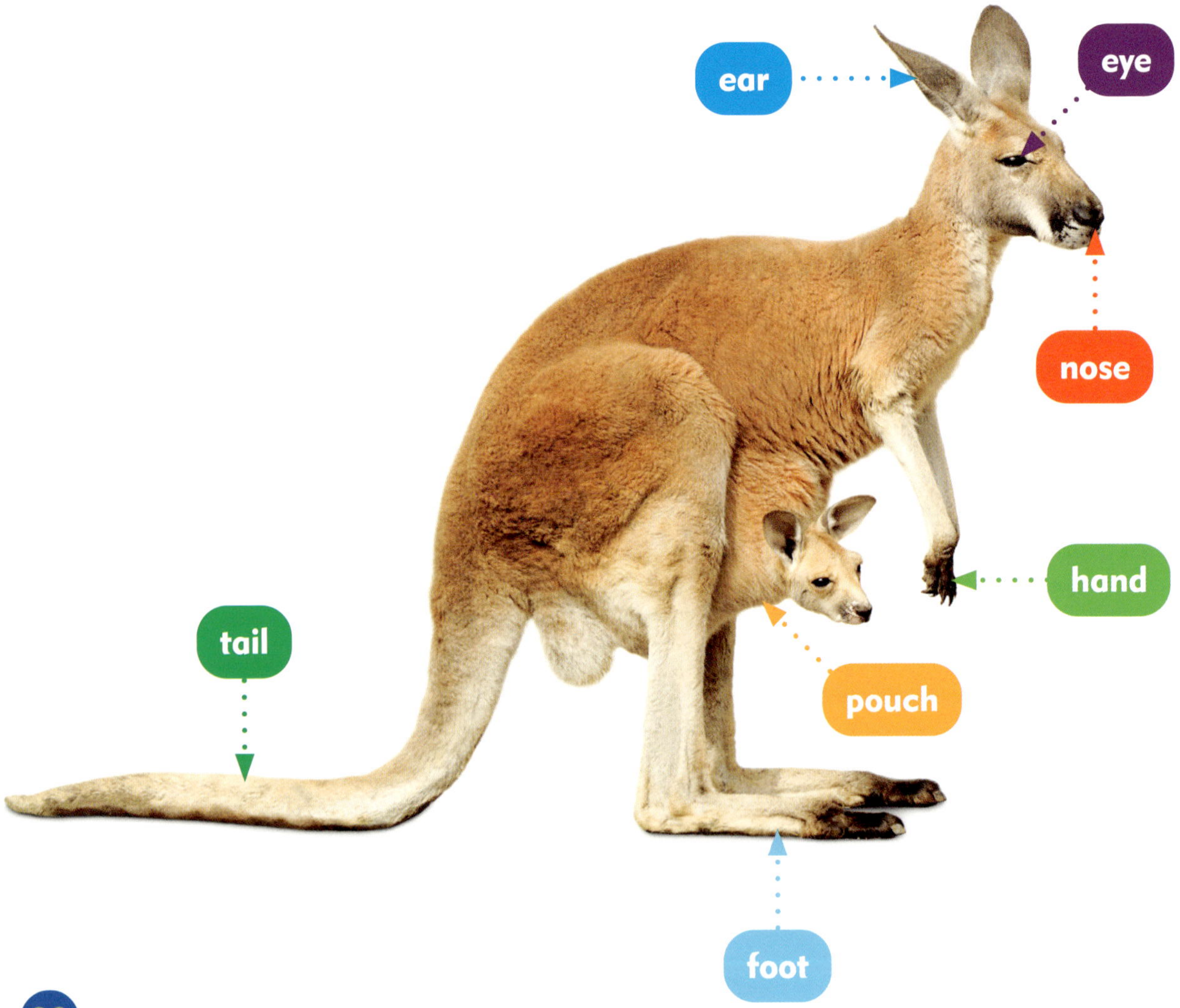

ear

eye

nose

hand

tail

pouch

foot

Picture Glossary

box
To fight with hands.

dingo
A type of wild dog that lives in Australia.

hunts
Chases and kills animals for food.

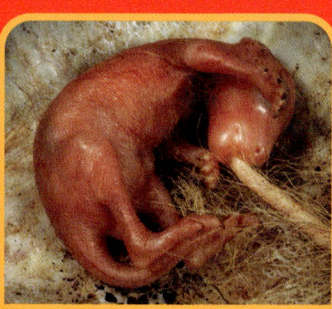

joey
A baby kangaroo.

mob
A group of kangaroos.

pouch
A pocket in a marsupial mother's body in which it carries its young.

Index

box 16
dingo 18
eat 9
feet 6
forests 8
grass 9
hop 4, 5, 19
joey 11, 15
mob 15
pouch 12, 15
sleep 21
tail 6

To Learn More

Finding more information is as easy as 1, 2, 3.

❶ Go to www.factsurfer.com

❷ Enter "kangaroos" into the search box.

❸ Choose your book to see a list of websites.